I0163016

Wild Animals of Kenya

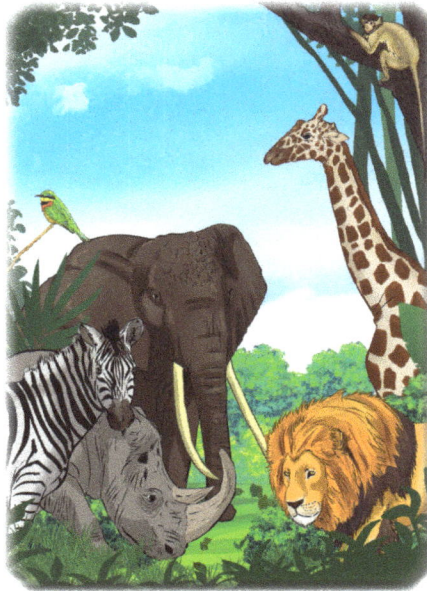

By Alex Kimathi

Illustrated by Anthony 'Mbembe' Zaza

Library For All Ltd.

Zebra

3

Giraffe

Hippo

Leopard

Snake

Bird

Crocodile

Monkey

Rhino

Elephant

Lion

About the contributors

Library For All works with authors and illustrators from around the world to develop diverse, relevant, high-quality books. Visit libraryforall.org for the latest news on writers' workshop events, submission guidelines and other creative opportunities.

Did you enjoy this book?

We have hundreds more expertly curated original stories to choose from.

We work in partnership with authors, educators, cultural advisors, governments and NGOs to bring the joy of reading to people everywhere.

Did you know?

We create global impact in these fields by embracing the United Nations Sustainable Development Goals.

3 GOOD HEALTH AND WELL-BEING	4 QUALITY EDUCATION	5 GENDER EQUALITY
8 DECENT WORK AND ECONOMIC GROWTH	9 INDUSTRY, INNOVATION AND INFRASTRUCTURE	10 REDUCED INEQUALITIES	11 SUSTAINABLE CITIES AND COMMUNITIES
12 RESPONSIBLE CONSUMPTION AND PRODUCTION	13 CLIMATE ACTION	16 PEACE, JUSTICE AND STRONG INSTITUTIONS	17 PARTNERSHIPS FOR THE GOALS

libraryforall.org

You're reading Level 1

Learner – Beginner readers

Start your reading journey with short words, big ideas and plenty of pictures.

Level 1 – Rising readers

Raise your reading level with more words, simple sentences and exciting images.

Level 2 – Eager readers

Enjoy your reading time with familiar words, but complex sentences.

Level 3 – Progressing readers

Develop your reading skills with creative stories and some challenging vocabulary.

Level 4 – Fluent readers

Step up your reading skills with playful narratives, new words and fun facts.

Level 5 – Curious readers

Discover your world through science and stories.

Level 6 – Adventurous readers

Explore your world through science and stories.

Original illustrations by Anthony 'Mbembe' Zaza

Wild Animals of Kenya
Kimathi, Alex
ISBN: 978-1-923339-20-0
SKU04516